Dr. D. K. Olukoya

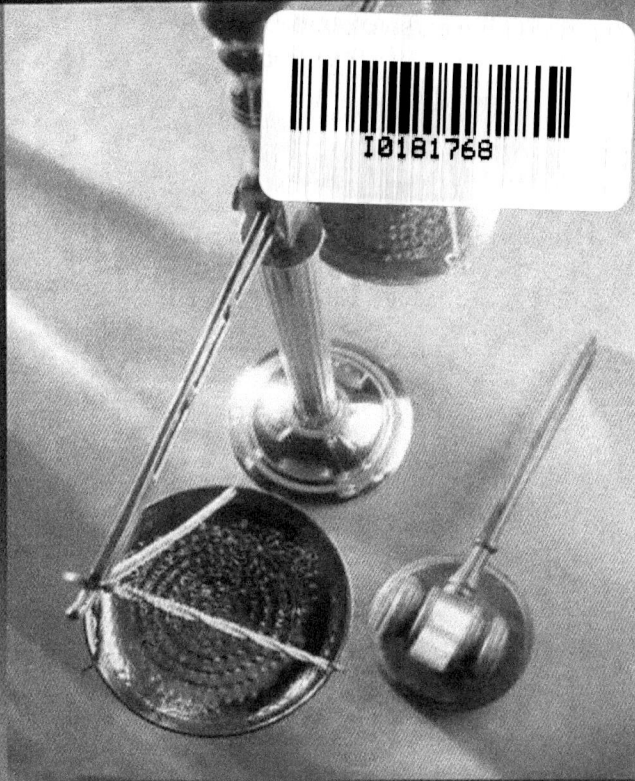

The Scale of
THE ALMIGHTY

The
SCALE
of the
ALMIGHTY

Dr. D.K Olukoya

1

THE SCALE OF THE ALMIGHTY
© 2011 DR. D. K. OLUKOYA
ISBN 978-978-49178-7-2
Copyright January 2011

Published by:
The Battle Cry Christian Ministries
322, Herbert Macaulay Way, Yaba P. O. Box 12272, Ikeja, Lagos.
email: battlecrysales@mountainoffire.org
Phone: 2348033044239

I salute my wonderful wife, Pastor Shade, for her invaluable support in the ministry.

I appreciate her unquantifiable support in the book ministry as the cover designer, art editor and art advisor

All Scripture quotation is from the King James Version of the Bible

CONTENTS

The Scale of the Almighty   5 - 13

The Divine Parameters   15 - 20

Weighed and Found Wanting   21 - 27

The Graveyard Church   29 - 35

The Turning Point   35 - 44

Challenging the Unchallengable   45 - 57

The scale of the Almighty

4

CHAPTER ONE

THE SCALE OF THE ALMIGHTY

It is one thing to call yourself something; it is another thing for God to call you something. You may decide to call yourself a pastor or an apostle or an evangelist, but in the book of God, which is the only book that matters, He may write that you are a messenger. It is not what you call yourself that matters but what God calls you.

> "Belshazzar the king made a great feast to a thousand of his lords, and drank wine before the thousand. Belshazzar, whiles he tasted the wine, commanded to bring the golden and silver vessels which his father Nebuchadnezzar had taken out of the temple, which was in Jerusalem; that the king, and his princes, his wives, and his concubines, might drink therein". **Daniel 5:1-2.**

WHEN PEOPLE GO TOO FAR
The party went on for a long time. Then all of a sudden, probably because of the effect of the alcohol, the king ordered his servants to bring the vessels that were taken from the temple in Jerusalem. At that level, he overstepped his bounds. He went too far.

A person can go too far. He can push himself to a level where the Spirit of God no longer strives, a level where God gives up on him. At a time the spirit will be urging you to pray, read the Bible, watch your temper, etc. But a time will come when the spirit would no longer strive with you. Once a person gets to that level, destruction is certain. I pray that such will not be your lot, in Jesus' name.

"*Then they brought the golden vessels that were taken out of the temple of the house of God which was at Jerusalem; and the king, and his princes, his wives, and his concubines, drank in them. They drank wine, and praised the gods of gold, and of silver, of brass, of iron, of wood, and of stone. In the same hour came forth fingers of a man's hand, and wrote over against the candlestick upon the plaister of the wall of the king's palace: and the king saw the part of the hand that wrote. Then the king's countenance was changed, and his thoughts troubled him, so that the joints of his loins were loosed, and his knees smote one against another. The king cried aloud to bring in the astrologers, the Chaldeans, and the soothsayers. And the king spake, and said to the wise men of Babylon, Whosoever shall read this writing, and shew me the interpretation thereof, shall be clothed with scarlet, and have a chain of gold about his neck, and shall be the third ruler in the kingdom*". **Daniel 5:3-7.**

"*Then came in all the king's wise men: but they could not read the writing, nor make known to the king the interpretation thereof. [9] Then was king Belshazzar greatly troubled, and his*

7

countenance was changed in him, and his lords were astonied". **Daniel 5:8-9**

They brought Daniel who said in **Daniel 5:25-28.**

"And this is the writing that was written, MENE, MENE, TEKEL, UPHARSIN. This is the interpretation of the thing: Mene; God hath numbered thy kingdom, and finished it. Tekel; Thou art weighed in the balances, and art found wanting. Peres; Thy kingdom is divided, and given to the Medes and Persians". **Daniel 5:25-28.**

THE PERFECT BALANCE

At the time Daniel was interpreting the writing, it was too late for the king to change the situation. Those who would destroy his kingdom were already banging at the door. He had gone down on the scale of the Almighty. He had failed completely on the balance of God.

We are in the habit of making one mistake or the other when we weigh things. But there is one balance in heaven which is absolutely perfect. It does not make mistakes. A pastor could make a mistake. He may say that you are the best person around and give you a spiritual assignment. But here is a balance in heaven which never makes mistakes. Other balances can get out of order. Their chains may break or one thing or the other may go wrong, so that when you measure something and it says it is one kilogram it may be less a little bit or more. But the balance of God never fails in its judgement. In God's balance one kilogram is one kilogram. No mistakes.

BABYLON THE GREAT

The incident we are discussing happened in the kingdom of Babylon. Babylon was a paradise of architecture. In fact, of all the kingdoms or empires in the world, there was none greater in splendour than Babylon. The most elaborate structures of modern times that we see are mere shadows of what was found in Babylon. The most sophisticated architectural designs of these days would not compare to those in Babylon before its fall. Millions of men were employed to build the walls around the city which was 60 miles in circumference and had 25 gates of solid brass on each side of the square city. Some houses in Babylon did not join one another on the ground, but a bridge passed from house to house. It had many fantastic structures, but as beautiful as it was, when it was weighed on the scale of God, it was found wanting and it fell.

GOD OF KNOWLEDGE

Our God has the knowledge that is beyond human reasoning. His ways of doing things are very strange to the human mind. He has His own way of detecting counterfeit or genuine services. If the service you are rendering to Him now is counterfeit, He knows how to measure it. If it is for show, He knows. If you are just an actor, when He puts your acting on the balance, it will go down.

Many years ago, a sister prayed certain prayer points and God told her to just watch and see. All of a sudden, she saw a picture of the rapture and everybody was being caught up. She was looking but could not go up, although she attended a Bible college. At first she thought it might be because she was fat, but when she looked up she saw people who were double her size being raptured. She tried to jump but something held her. She started to cry and an angel of God came to her and said, " I want to show you your mark on the balance of the Almighty." The angel gave her a piece of paper which read 22 per cent. Her score was inadequate, so she could not go anywhere.

HEAVEN'S TEST
When you are serving the Lord, He runs your service through fire. He has his own method of testing you. According to 1 Corinthians 3:13, if you are sinning, it will be made manifest.   If you are preaching, it will be made manifest. Whatever you are doing would manifest. If you like, do the work of God deceitfully, it shall be made manifest. If you like, be stealing materials from the house of God. It shall be made manifest. The day shall declare it because it shall be revealed by fire which shall try every man's work.

> "And he called unto him his disciples, and saith unto them, Verily I say unto you, That this poor widow hath cast more in, than all they which

10

*have cast into the treasury: For all they did cast
in of their abundance; but she of her want did
cast in all that she had, even all her living".*
Mark 12:43-44.

God measures your tithes and offerings by the amount you keep
for yourself. So, you must take heed to yourself so that you do not
offer the gospel to others while you remain a stranger. Take heed
so that you do not become a human signboard or spiritual tout,
shouting various bus-stops, but never trying to take a seat inside
the bus. Be careful, beloved, that you do not perish while you are
warning others not to perish.

GOD'S STANDARD
Take heed so that after warning others to run away from hell fire,
you do not enter the place yourself. Do not be a tailor who goes
about in rags while you are cutting and sewing clothes for people
every day. Think about it. God has his own way of measurement.
He took three million Jews into the wilderness and took just two
to the Promised Land. As far as His judgement was concerned,
that was a success. Men would say, what a fantastic failure? But
God was not worried. After all the Bible says that God would not
mind turning a whole nation into hell fire if necessary.

There is the story of a brother who was interpreting in the church
and suddenly fell down and died. His wife sent to his people to
come and bury him. On the fourth day, when they came to collect
his body from the mortuary, they found tears in his eyes and all of
a sudden, he opened his eyes and started talking. He said that

immediately he died, he found himself in a pit of darkness, that the darkness was so thick that you could cut it with a knife. But inside there was a narrow path, so narrow that it took one leg to move at a time.

THE NARROW PATH

The brother said that by the side of the narrow path was a wide road and there were lots of people in it, but at the end of it was a big hole burning with fire. He said that the rate at which people, including school children, were going inside was as if a tipper was dropping sand. But he did not find another person on the narrow path which, he said, led to a very high mountain.

He said that occasionally he would nearly fall but something would appear before him and say, "Do not fall." And he kept moving until he got to the top where there were angels who had one small television set the size of a shoe polish can. He said that immediately one arrived there the angels asked his name. On mentioning his name, every sin he had committed, right from when he was an infant, would appear on the television set.

He said that at a stage while the angels were relaying the sins of a certain man, including the incest he committed with his younger sister, the man cried: "Please, switch it off, I don't want to look at it again. Switch it off because it is terrible." However, anything that you confessed and called the blood of Jesus to cleanse would not be shown, unless you went back to the sin.

When the angels switched off the television set and asked the man, "What is in your pocket?" he put his hand in his pocket and brought out anger. The angels said, "Since you call yourself a Christian, how come these things are still in your life?" The man said, "I am sorry, it is the devil." They shouted, "Lucifer" All of a sudden, Lucifer showed up, laughing.

WHERE DO YOU STAND?
The brother said he also heard the scream of another sister who died in his church about three years back and who used to sing a special number. This sister was boiling and shouting with soprano voice in hell fire. When the brother heard it he started crying. That was when he was shedding the tears that his people saw at the mortuary.

If the Lord begins to weigh you today, where do you stand? That rich man said, "My soul, rejoice and be glad, I still have many years." But God said, "This night your soul shall be taken away from you." When you are gone, all the things you have gathered, to whom will they belong? All you have acquired by running around restlessly, who will have them when you are gone?

I have often said that there are two places where sermons are effective: the cemetery and the lepers' colony. In fact, one of the best altar calls I have seen was at the cemetery. The preacher began: "Three days ago, this man was drinking Coke in my house I did not know that in three days time he would have gone. But he is here now. One day, whether you like it or not, whether you refuse to grow old or not, whether you are polishing your nails and carrying your body cream everywhere you go, one day you will land here too. And other people will say, Oh, he has gone home. But who knows where you are going? Who really knows?"

CHAPTER TWO

THE DIVINE PARAMETERS

The balance of God can weigh men and determine their integrity.
Job 31:6 says:
"Let me be weighed in an even balance, that God may know mine integrity."

God's balance can weigh men of low degree and high degree.

> *"Truly my soul waiteth upon God: from him cometh my salvation".* **Psalm 62:1.**

VANITY!

Vanity is zero. But the scripture says that somebody can weigh less than zero. There are many l ike that in the house of God. God is weighing you. He is looking at you. You are taking Him for a ride. That is because the Bible says that He does not want anybody to perish. He is long suffering. So you take Him for granted.

SPIRITUAL GOATS

Recently, before a particular girl d ied she came to see me, and she wrote a l ist of 40 men she had slept with. What pained me most was the last man. He was the one who converted her to Christ in a hol iness-preaching church. The man slept with her, a new convert, not knowing that she had HIV. So, he signed a death sentence for himself. The same brother would jump forward and scream, "Without hol iness, no man shall see God." He would come forward and say, "Hol iness is our watchword" and would sing in bass tone. But God is weighing him. All his songs will stand against him on the day of judgement. He will be asked, "Did you not sing these songs? Did you understand what you were singing?" He may reply, "I sang. I understood." The angels may now ask him, "Then what happened?" He may say, "I don't know." The angles will say, "Get him away. Let him join the goats at the left side."

In any church there are two groups of people: the goats and the sheep. The goats go to the left hand while the lambs go to the right hand. A lamb does what you want it to do. It appears like a fool, but it does not perish easily as the goat.

GOD'S WEIGHING SCALE
God can weigh men of low degree and those of high degree. Eventually, some of the big men will realise that in heaven, unlike in the world, there is no first class person. Things are not done there the way they are done here. No angel can change what he has written about you because you say, "When I was in the world, I was living in a reserved area." God is weighing you everyday. If a person allows himself to get to zero level, the devil will come quickly and kill him and he will go to hell.

God's balance can weigh the paths and the ways of men. It can weigh your path, the way you go, all the people you visit, the kind of relationship you have with your fiancée, etc. So, you can see that the balance of the Lord is very interesting. It is the same balance that is written about in Job 28:25:
"To make the weight for the winds; and he weigheth the waters by measure."
Proverbs 16:2 also says:
> *"All the ways of a man are clean in his own
> eyes; but the Lord weigheth the spirits."*

17

God's balance weighs many things. David's father had many sons. Some were huge and handsome and some looked respectable and holy. They seem qualified to be the king of Israel and Samuel almost made a mistake when he saw Eliab coming. He said, "Surely, this is he." But the Lord said to him, "Look not at his countenance, nor at his frame, for the Lord looketh not as man looketh. Man looketh at the surface but I, the Lord, look at the heart." So, God had looked at the heart of all the sons of Jesse, weighed all of them and only David measured up to the standard. In fact, David had not been called. He was the smallest son and was looking after the sheep.

Samuel said, "Go and bring him. We will not sit down till he comes." And he remained standing with his anointing oil looking for the head to pour it on. Many people lift up their hands and pray, "Anointing fall on me." Some of them are goats and the heavens are saying: "You want anointing, but there are horns on your head. Break the horns, so that you can become a lamb. Then we can anoint you."

CONFLICTING SPIRITS
One goat would say, "No, anointing must fall on me." The heavens would say, "Okay, since we said, break your horns and you refuse, we will pour the oil on your horns." Then the person will begin false prophecy. He would pray but two spirits will be quarrelling inside him. He would be preaching to thousands of people and at the same time he would be sleeping with a spirit wife. Two forces would combine themselves in his life. He would sit down and read the Bible up to the point that people will be saying that he is running mad. But at the same time when he sleeps, he would be playing with masquerades. So there are two conflicting things in his life.

God can also weigh your spirit. **1 Samuel 2:3** says:

*"Talk no more so exceeding proudly; let not
arrogancy come out of your mouth: for the Lord
is a God of knowledge, and by him actions are
weighed."*

EXAMINE YOURSELF

Beloved, if you want to experience the power that the apostles
experienced, you should examine yourself carefully. If God were
to weigh your spirit now, do you think that you are up to the
required standard? Some raise their hands everyday and pray, "God
heal me, heal me, I will serve you till I die." And God says, "Okay,
receive your healing." They received the healing and that is the
last day you see them in the church.

ARE YOU UP TO STANDARD?

God weighs our actions. If He weighs your actions now, do you
think you will be up to the standard? The scarcity of the power of
God in any generation is not the fault of God, but the unavailability
of men and women that He can use. By the time God grabs a
person and says, "I want to use this one," He has seen that it is the
kind of person He can use. If God was to weigh your integrity as a
Christian, are you up to the standard? This is the question you
need to ask yourself.

One of our ministers prayed for a certain rich man who had
a bad leg and the Lord healed him. Later, the rich man gave
the minister a very nice brief case which he was carrying
about proudly. One day, he offended the rich man and he
began to speak against the minister and reported him to

me. He said, "My wife used to prepare tea for this pastor. She used to do this or that for him. I used to carry him about in my car. He is an ungrateful person. I gave him a brief case."

At a point the pastor said, "G.O, what can I do? I said, "This is why I warn you pastors running around some rich people. You see yourself now? Prostrate and beg him." The pastor prostrated saying, "I am sorry, sir." The man said, "It is all right. You can stand up." This was the person who had no leg to walk and now he could walk.

ACTIVITIES OF DEVOURERS

If God were to measure your financial contributions, do you think you would be up to the standard? Somebody prayed and the Lord blessed him with 20,000 dollars but to pay the tithe of 2,000 dollars was hard for him. He said "It is hard." Of course, the Lord allowed the devil to create problems that made him spent the money. Devourers were released upon the money that he had thought was heavy.

For a person to steal from God he must be a fantastic thief and a dangerous person to live with. If your husband is stealing from God, you have married a dangerous man. If your business is stealing from God, it will soon become a graveyard, unless you quickly do a restitution. If God were to weigh your financial contribution, where would you go? If you are a student pay tithe on your pocket money. If not, a simple sickness can squander the pocket money.

CHAPTER THREE

WEIGHED
AND
FOUND WANTING

If God were to weigh your zeal for lost souls, will you be up to the standard? If God were to weigh your spiritual activities in the church, do you think they will be up to the standard? If God were to weigh your love to others, do you think it will be up to his standard? If God were to weigh your zeal for the house of God, do you think it will be up to His standard? Human beings may be dishonest about their balances, and their measurement cups. You can knock your cup inside, but not God's. The balances of God will not make mistakes.

"Thou art weighed and found wanting", were the words that came to Belshazzar. You may be born in a church or dedicated in a house of God. Your father may be a pastor, your mother may be a prophetess. But the day you are found wanting on God's scale, that is it. Belshazzar did not get a second chance. His time was up. He had gone too far. His mistakes were many.

SIPPING SAINTS?
He lived in pleasure and alcohol, just as some people who come to church are still drinking and saying: "I'm not a heavy drinker. The Bible does not say, "Don't drink, it says don't get drunk." Is that really what the Bible says? Such people are putting a curse on themselves. The Bible says, "If you want to be a prophet of God, a priest unto God, you should not drink. But if you want to perish drink."
The book of Revelation says that if after you have read it and you decide to be doing evil, continue and if you decide to be doing good, continue. But behold, Jesus is coming quickly and His

reward is with Him to give to every man according to his works. This means that after reading it you may continue in iniquity. The Bible says "Give wine to those who want to perish." If you insist on taking alcoholic drinks, all the prayer point, "I fire back every arrow of witchcraft", you are praying is only a joke. Demons will say, "Which arrow is he firing back? He drinks the arrow every night."

ALCOHOL ADDICTS

Belshazzar loves alcohol and parties. There are some people who like going to parties. Some do not go but would send their children. Some put on their little girls trousers and earrings that they themselves do not wear and send them to parties. The earrings could be those they inherited from their grandmothers who died of cancer. They push their teenage daughters to parties and they come back and say, "This is my boyfriend." You now say, "No, don't say that kind of thing in our family." But you urged her to go to the party.

Sometimes ago, a woman dragged her daughter who was under 15 to me saying, "This one is not serious. She doesn't pray at home. When we pray she sleeps." Immediately I was about to pray, the Holy Spirit said, "She's not sick. She's pregnant" I told her mother that she was not sick the reason she could not pray was that she was pregnant. The woman screamed. I said, "Madam, don't cry. Even you, you are with your fifth husband, so she just collected your anointing." When she heard me, she stopped crying.

Belshazzar cared very little about God. He decided to insult God. He was a proud man. He said, "Art thou Daniel of the Hebrew slaves that my father brought?" Daniel would have said, "Yes, I am

Daniel. But listen, I am not interested in becoming the third in command. The kingdom will fall anyway. Your father, Nebuchadnezzar, suffered. God threw him into the forest to suffer for seven years and made him eat grass like animals so that he might know that God is the ruler of men. You, the son, you were alive there. You saw it and in spite of the fact that you saw it you refuse to learn from your fathers mistakes. So the hand that wrote the Ten Commandments of Moses now comes down."

There are two sins that the Bible says cannot be forgiven:

1. **Sin against the Holy Spirit.**
2. **Wilful sin.**

Sin against the Holy Spirit will attract punishment, sometimes without remedy. When the Holy Spirit says, "Thus saith the Lord" and you say, "No, I will not follow it" or "Thus saith the Lord and you say, "It is a demon that is saying it," there would be no remedy for your punishment.

If you offend the Father, the Son will beg for you. If you offend the Son, you can ask the Holy Spirit for your forgiveness. But if you offend the Holy Spirit, you are finished. Belshazzar knew all these things but continued in sin. Do you know that many churchgoers are like that? Since I got born again, I have learnt something from counselling. The sins that glue people to themselves are fornication and adultery. Such people feel sorry for themselves while hearing the word of God, only to fall back into sin soon after.. Wilful sin will also attract punishment and sometimes without remedy.

24

Forget the notion that it is only han ᵈsome men and beautiful women that commit fornication. No, that spirit has nothing to do with aesthetic values. Sometimes, it is easier to get a witch delivered because once that anointing of fornication and adultery comes upon a man, he forgets that the person is his house help. He forgets that and you don't have control over your thoughts, your balance may be reading zero.

ZERO WEIGHT

If your spiritual life is going up and down, your balance may be reading zero. If your main purpose of coming to the house of God is for prosperity and protection, your balance may be reading zero. If you are not interested in soul-wining, your balance may be reading zero. If you have been avoiding paying your tithes or you have people you don't greet or you keep malice against, or you live a life of fornication, your balance is reading zero.

If we have to go back to our roots, we must go back to the foundation and bring quality repentance unto the Lord, so that we can become what He wants us to become. Talk to the Lord about your life. Say: "Lord what do I have? Where do I stand? I may have been calling myself one thing and you are calling me another. I don't want to continue to live for nothing. Time is going. I am not getting any younger. Something must happen in my life. I know that this is not the best you have for me."

It can be very sad if you have been coming to the meetings of the old pathway and your life has not started to move in the old path. Settle it before the Lord.

A GOAT OR A LAMB?

I have seen many people in the spirit struggling. If only they would allow the Lord to break off the horns of the goat so that they will become a lamb. The enemy holding onto that horn will have no more horn to hold. It is because there is horn on their head that the battle is still strong. The day you become what God wants you to become, all the warfare that you are fighting will surely come to an end and you will have victory over your enemy. The enemy will have no hiding place in your life again. But when you prepare a loophole for the enemy, he will take full position.

The Psalmist says, "The day that I cried unto the Lord, then shall my enemy turn back, this I know, for God is with me." The reason some people are doing deliverance upon deliverance is that they refuse to depart from their sins. Some people will say, "Well, by the grace of God, I am living a life of holiness." Yet there is malice in their lives. Holy life and there are some people they don't greet. Holy life when they are just holding their anger inside. Holy life and they are still stealing money where they work. Holy life and when they borrow money from the cooperative they don't want to pay. Holy life when they buy things on credit and refuse to pay back. Don't deceive yourself. Repent and your life will not remain the same.

PRAYER POINTS

1. Lord, deliver me from the spirit of hell fire, in the name of Jesus.
2. Lord, show me where I stand, in the name of Jesus.
3. My inner man, receive fire in Jesus' name.
4. Every witchcraft deposit in my life, die, in Jesus' name.
5. Every power pursuing me out of the way of life, die, in Jesus' name.

CHAPTER FOUR

THE
GRAVEYARD
CHURCH

You may wonder if there is anything like the graveyard church. You may wish to ask or perhaps to establish the difference between a church and a graveyard. There are lots of strange things happening in these last days. There are lots of dead men and women in the sanctuary.

The church as you know it, is a place of worship for the living, while the graveyard is the final resting place for the physically dead people. It then follows that if a church were built in a graveyard, no activity would take place therein.

THE CHURCH OF SARDIS

"And unto the angel of the church in Sardis write; These things saith he that hath the seven Spirits of God, and the seven stars; I know thy works, that thou hast a name that thou livest, and art dead Be watchful, and strengthen the things which remain, that are ready to die: for I have not found thy works perfect before God Remember therefore how thou hast received and heard, and hold fast, and repent. If therefore thou shalt not watch, I will come on thee as a thief, and thou shalt not know what hour I will come upon thee Thou hast a few names even in Sardis, which have not defiled their garments; and they shall walk with me in white: for they are worthy He that overcometh, the same shall be clothed in white raiment; and I will not blot out his name out of the book of life, but I will confess his name before my Father, and before his angels,

30

He that hath an ear, let him hear what the
Spirit saith unto the churches." **Rev 3:1-6.**

Verses one to six were particularly addressed to the church of
Sardis. The Bible says that the church had a name. But as far as
God was concerned, that church was diseased.

WHAT GOD CALLS YOU
When you look at this fact very closely, you will find that it is not
what you call yourself that actually matters, but what God calls
you. It is possible for you to call yourself an angel, but as far as God
is concerned He thinks differently about you. The Lord said that
that church had a name once but was dead thereafter. It follows
that it would no longer function as it used to be. A dead person
will behave like the dead and a living person as the living. While
some people in the churches today are spiritually awake, others
are spiritually dead. The latter are those the Bible refers to as dead
people.

A quick look at the word of God will tell you that it talks about five groups
of spiritually dead people. If however the Bible regards one as dead and
one regards oneself as living, then one is deceiving oneself. The groups of
dead people are as follows:
1. THE BACKSLIDERS
> They are those who have stopped following the Lord the
> way He should be followed. They are people whose spiritual
> lives are now very weak. Indeed they are people who find it
> difficult to pray and study the word of God. They find
> it difficult to witness to others about the Lord Jesus

31

Christ. But the Lord is now asking spiritual sleepers to wake up. He is also challenging the spiritually dead people to rise up. As far as the Lord is concerned backsliders or spiritual sleepers are dead.

2. SINNERS

All sinners are spiritually dead. The day a sinner becomes alive is the day he repents from his sins and cries for forgiveness. When that happens, such a sinner has become aware that he was dead and needed to give his life to the Lord Jesus to come alive. All sinners, as far as the Bible is concerned, are dead people.

3. THE CARNALLY MINDED

"For to be carnally minded is death; but to be spiritually minded is life and peace". **Romans 8:6**

It follows therefore that a person who is always thinking of carnal things is dead while still alive. Such a person is not interested in how you can grow spiritually. He or she is only interested in how to make more money and to become more comfortable. A carnal mind is an abomination to God, that is why the Bible says that to be carnally minded is death.

4. THE HATERS OF KNOWLEDGE

The fourth group of dead people are found in **Proverbs 21:6**:
"The getting of treasures by a lying tongue is a vanity tossed to and fro of them that seek death."

These are those who are not interested in learning more about the Lord Jesus Christ. They are just comfortable or contended with how they are spiritually. Such people think they have got it all.

5. PLEASURE SEEKERS

The last group of spiritually dead people are found in 1 Tim. 5:6

"But she that liveth in pleasure is dead while she liveth".

As far as the Bible is concerned, pleasure seekers are only happy when there are lots of singing and dancing and entertainment around. They re dead people! As far as the Bible is concerned they are not even qualified to praise God.

It is amazing that many have not known this fact, that spiritually dead people are not qualified to praise the Lord. Psalm 115:17 says:

> *"The dead praise not the Lord, neither any that go down into silence."*

Isaiah 38:19 says:

> *"The living, the living, he shall praise thee, as I do this day: the father to the children shall make known thy truth."*

Thus dead people are not qualified to praise God. Dead churches are not qualified to praise the Lord too. Such people should not expect anything that will last from God! In fact the Bible says that they are not even qualified to handle the word of God.

Beloved, I would like you to close your eyes where you are now and quietly examine your spirit.

Perhaps you have been classifying yourself wrongly. Perhaps you are not aware that you are not in the classification of the Almighty God. Begin to talk to the Lord at this moment. Ask the Holy Spirit to give you the true picture of your life today. Talk to the Lord now.

WHEN DEMONS SPEAK
I do hope you have not forgotten a memorable story which involves Paul in Acts 16-19. While Paul was preaching the word of God in Philippians, a certain damsel who had the spirit of divination from the devil kept following him and prophesying that Paul and his ministers were servants of the most high God sent to preach salvation to the people. Although she was saying the correct thing, Paul, nonetheless, had to keep her quiet. The reason he did that was to ensure that an unworthy vessel possessed by satanic spirit does not speak the word of God. Little wonder then that he rebuked the spirit in the girl and commanded it to depart from her right at that moment.

Know this fact therefore that the lady could not be allowed to handle the word of God because she was not spiritually fit.

Many people stubbornly sit tight in their dead churches and many take solace in their dead environment. It is such places that household enemies will ensure that such people are given church posts to tie them down. They would never be able to attend a living church where they would be saved. When such people are told to pray, they would start naming their church posts instead of praying. The devil has deceitfully planted things in them. It is an evidence of life that is not alive to God at all.

CHAPTER FIVE

THE
TURNING POINT

I need to tell you my story in this chapter. A long time ago, I was attending a very big church; I was an organist as well as a choirmaster of the church. The church bought a big organ practically because of me and was even indebted, because of the organ. They promised me heaven on earth in that particular church and I resumed my choirmaster job in full as soon as I returned from England. The turning point came, however, with a night vision.

A VISION

In a vision one night, I saw something terrible. A tall, black man was standing right at the middle of the church and all of us in the church that were very prayerful and did not like the way things were going on in the church started fighting him with horse whips. Each person had a horse whip in his hand and was beating him with all his strength. But the more we beat him the stronger he became. At a stage we conferred together on what to do next and concluded that he was the cause of the trouble in the church. However, somebody in that vision observed that the black man demon was not affected because the horse-whip we were using was not effective. To confirm this, we decided to test the horse whip on the body of one of us, but as we beat him blood started oozing out of his body. Then the man we were fighting started laughing at us, that although we had come to fight him we were fighting one another.

THE VOICE OF THE LORD

Then the voice of the Lord came to me in the vision very audibly that He did not ask me to stay in that church. Of course, I had to leave the church immediately. Thereafter, about six of us started fellowship meetings in a small shop. People laughed at me and in fact ridiculed me that if I had read mathematics they would have thought that I was mad. They wondered how I could leave a big church to fellowship in a small shop with six people.

I thank God that I did not listen to them. For if I had, there would not have been the Mountain of Fire and Miracles Ministries today. What answer would I have given for the blood of numberless believers I would have had on my head?

DEAD CHURCH
The lesson to be learnt here is that taking up a post in a dead church is tantamount to voting for the graveyard. Numberless people are tied down with church posts. I hope you know the fact that, whatever effort a police man puts at a burial ground to look after the dead is a useless exercise.

They make people churchwardens of the dead, choirmasters for the dead, patron for the dead, matrons for the dead, etc. All such posts are to ensure the deaths of such people themselves.

If somebody is spiritually dead, he does not see the way any longer. He may not know the place he is in until the Spirit of God departs from him.
I was going to a church before, where all we did on Sundays was dancing, clapping our hands and singing. We also jumped on the benches. After we have done all that the pastor would announce that our time was far spent and therefore he would not be able to preach any sermon. But we had enough time for endless offerings and thereafter we would say the grace and go home. While we

were busy doing that, the devil was not only rejoicing but also planting endless calamities among us.

I was going to that church until one day something happened to me which shook me out of it. Somebody was boiling oil on fire and I was sitting nearby reading my book. Suddenly, before my very eyes, part of the oil on fire became a ball and flew to my direction and fell on my leg. I could not move and I cried out to the entire household for help. The first person who came said, "Let us pour ice water on his legs," another person said, "Let us put pap," and another pleaded that they should put egg. While my leg was burning, they were busy arguing untill they agreed on what to do.

Within two months my left hand broke. So I had a broken hand and a roasted leg. One night, the Lord came to me and warned me that I would end up being killed in the dead church. He told me that if I had been attending a living church I would have been able to reject calamities that befell me. It was from that time that I started calling on the name of the Lord the way it should be called. He heard me and promoted me from my terrible spiritual position to the top of the rock.

DEAD BELIEVERS
The problem of the church today is that many hypocrites are now there. They refuse to leave their sins and their dead churches. The Lord cannot help such people.

You do not do the work of the Lord deceitfully. You cannot cheat God. If you do, you will pay for it.

40

YOUR SPIRITUAL CONDITION

If you hide your spiritual condition, God will leave you to your problems. If you are struggling to do some other things that you are not supposed to do, you must do something about it, for God is concerned about you.

If the trumpet of the Lord should sound today, the evidence that you are in good church is that you will reign with Christ.

A lot of people are too worldly to be useful spiritually. They are afraid or ashamed of being tagged fanatical for Jesus. But the truth is that the Lord expects a believer to be fanatical.

So many people do not want to serve the Lord because of certain things in their lives which they do not want to drop. They are afraid that if they join the Christian fold, they would no longer be able to do such things that please them. Those things have become idols for them. Anything at all that you cannot drop for the sake of God has become an idol in your life. If all you want to do is to please human beings, just too bad.

When the time of rapture comes these people you are seeking to please, will not be able to help you at all. They are totally useless as far as spiritual help is concerned.

WHEN YOU ARE DEAD

Why should you design your life after the thoughts and the love of the people of the world? Why should a child of hell fire decide your dress pattern for you? How could he be the one to tell you whether or not you are looking fine or dull? Even if you are looking dull, is that the business of a child of hell-fire? If he says you are looking dull and heaven says you are looking bright, won't you be happy? Immediately you begin to live the type of life the Lord wants you to live you will invite enemies automatically to yourself. Nobody would have the guts to invite you to worldly parties again, the moment you are God-crazy. Even if they had put your name unknowingly they would definitely remove it.

You cannot be hot for God without becoming automatic enemies of people of the world. It is a pity, however, that some people compromise their faith so much to please people of darkness. When somebody is dead spiritually, good things that are spiritually inclined will not be opened to him or her.

A dead person cannot see God. Only a living person can serve the Lord Jesus Christ.

When everything is almost gone and all things are closing down, it is then that many people will realise how much debt they owe to the Lord. Many of such people will realise the vanity of the world in which their lives had been.

THE ACCOUNT
Each person will account individually for his or her stewardship on earth. Even couples will account individually. Therefore you cannot blame your husband, wife or children for your lack of spiritual development. If you seek pleasure alone while you are alive, you are indeed dead.

Why should believers follow unbelievers to their parties and help them to do their cooking? If you are still worshipping God in your sins, then you are not in any way different from members of the dead church of the Sardis, a church that was in the burial ground. Take a step of faith today by separating yourself from the churches or groups of the dead. Separate yourself in your mode of dressing, conversation, attitude, faith, way of life, etc. Quit from the congregation of the dead people today. It really does not pay you. The end thereof is eternal death. Are you still hot for God or have you started backsliding? Do you find it difficult to witness to others? Do you still harbour sins in your life?

Are you still carnally minded? Do you as a matter of fact lack the knowledge of the Lord Jesus Christ? Are you still a pleasure seeker? If your answers to these questions are yes, then you are spiritually dead. You are indeed one of the worshippers in the graveyard church. Repent of all your sins today and the Lord Jesus Christ will receive you with open arms back into His divine fold. Remember that you alone will give account of your stewardship. Shun every worldly shame and criticisms. Come to God and He will bless you mightily.

Note this: To be dead without Christ is hell! It is even more hellish to be spiritually dead without Christ. He who has ears to hear what God is saying at this end time, let him hear. Remember this fact that heaven will always listen to the cries of believers.

PRAYER POINTS
1. Let the Holy Spirit fill me afresh, in the name of Jesus.
2. Let every unbroken area in my life be broken, in the name of Jesus.

3. Father, incubate me with fire of the Holy Spirit, in Jesus' name.
4. Let every anti-power bondage break in my life, in the name of Jesus.
5. Let all strangers flee from my spirit and let the Holy Spirit take control, in Jesus' name.
6. Lord, catapult my spiritual life to the mountain top, in the name of Jesus.
7. Lord, fill me with spiritual gifts, in the name of Jesus.
8. Let heavens open and let the glory of God fall upon me, in the name of Jesus.
9. Let signs and wonders be my lot, in Jesus' name.
10. Let the joy of the oppressors over my life be turned into sorrow, in the name of Jesus.
11. Let all multiple strongmen operating against me be paralysed, in Jesus' name.
12. Lord, open my eyes and ears to receive wondrous things from You, in the name of Jesus.
13. Lord, grant me victory over every temptation and satanic device, in the name of Jesus.
14. Lord, ignite my spiritual life so that I will stop fishing in unprofitable waters, in the name of Jesus.
15. Lord, release the Pentecostal tongue of fire to burn in my life, family and ministry, in the name of Jesus.

CHAPTER SIX

CHALLENGING THE UNCHALLENGABLE

There is a very powerful word that men love a lot but few men have it. The word is POWER. Power is a very wonderful word. Although it may sound simple, it is nonetheless difficult to define. For example, keeping quiet in a particular situation may be seen as power. Talking in a particular situation can also mean power. Sometimes a person's attitude to a particular thing can be interpreted to mean power.

The word power can be defined in diverse ways. It can sometimes mean force or strength. It can also mean the ability to do something or to act on a particular issue. It could also mean the right to control other people or to exercise authority over others. But what does the Bible say about power? Let us check the scriptures to ascertain this. Second Chronicle. 32:7-8 has this interesting statement which Hezekiah uttered when Sennacherib, the king of Assyria, led his forces to attack him and his people:.

> "Be strong and courageous, be not afraid nor dismayed for the king of Assyria, nor for all the multitude that is with him: for there be more with us than with him: With him is an arm of flesh; but with us is the Lord our God to help us, and to fight our battles. And the people rested themselves upon the words of Hezekiah king of Judah". 2 Chronicle. 32:7-8

At this juncture, I would like you to confess this out with a loud voice, "There will be more with me than with my enemies."

THE ARM OF FLESH

It is an established fact that the arm of flesh cannot help anyone. That is why that popular song says: "Stand up, stand up for Jesus, *stand in His strength alone, the arm of flesh will fail you, you dare not trust your own."* Hezekiah knew that the arm of flesh could not save them, that it was only the Lord God that could fight their battles for them. Sennacherib rel ied on the arm of flesh and ruined himself.

Let us examine the Bible to fish out some other examples of those who trusted in the arm of flesh and their eventual tragedy. Nebuchadnezzar who headed one of the greatest kingdoms in the whole world boasted in his strength. He felt that none was l ike him in power and riches. He felt that as the emperor of the kingdom of Babylon and indeed of all empires that surrounded it, he was incomparable with anyone in terms of glory and fame. That was why he boasted in **Daniel 3:15:**

"Now if ye be ready that at what time ye hear the sound of the cornet, flute, harp, sackbut, psaltery, and dulcimer, and all kinds of music, ye fall down and worship the image which I have made; well: but if ye worship not, ye shall be cast the same hour into the midst of a burning fiery furnace; and who is that God that shall deliver you out of my hands?"

The foregoing shows us how muth Nebuchadnezzar trusted his arm of flesh. But when a superior power came into operation, he changed his tune.

> *"Then Nebuchadnezzar spake, and said, Blessed be the God of Shadrach, Meshach, and Abed-nego, who hath sent his angel, and delivered his servants that trusted in him, and have changed*

47

the king's word, and yielded their bodies, that they might not serve nor worship any god, except their own God. Therefore I make a decree, That every people, nation, and language, which speak any thing amiss against the God of Shadrach, Meshach, and Abed-nego, shall be cut in pieces, and their houses shall be made a dunghill: because there is no other God that can deliver after this sort". **Daniel 3:28-29:**

THE SUPERIOR POWER
Beloved, the arithmetic is simple: the arm of flesh must bow when it is confronted by the only Superior Power, which is the power of the Almighty God. Goliath is another example of a man who boasted openly about his power. After the battle line had been drawn between his forces and the forces of Saul, he boasted openly for 40 days, of his trust in his arm of flesh.

"And he stood and cried unto the armies of Israel, and said unto them, why are ye come out to set your battle in array? am not I a Philistine, and ye servants to Saul? Choose you a man for you, and let him come down to me. If he be able to fight with me, and to kill me, then will we be your servants: but if I prevail against him, and kill him, then shall ye be our servants, and serve us. And the Philistine said, I defy the armies of Israel this day; give me a man, that we may fight together". **1 Samuel 17:8-10:**

CARNAL BOASTS

While the boasting in the arm of flesh continued the whole army of Israel went into hiding. Saul, its leader who was taller from the shoulder than all Israelites, had to hide himself too. But at the eighth appearance of Goliath, which was on the 40th day, the superior power of God came into operation, through a small boy. Age is not a measurement of spirituality. It was a small boy who had the big God within him that posed a great challenge to Goliath. But Goliath was not done with his trust in the arm of flesh. He made another terrible statement in **1 Samuel 17:44:**

> *"And the Philistine said to David, Come to me,*
> *and I will give thy flesh unto the fowls of the*
> *air, and to the beasts of the field."*

THE DOOMSDAY

It was at that juncture that David made it clear to Goliath that his doomsday had come. In 1 Samuel 17:45. David made this interesting statement:

"Then said David to the Philistine, Thou comest to me with a sword, and with a spear, and with a shield: but I come to thee in the name of the Lord of hosts, the God of the armies of Israel, whom thou hast defied." **1 Samuel 17:45.**

The result of the challenge can be found in **1 Samuel 17:49-50:**

"And David put his hand in his bag, and took thence a stone, and slang it, and smote the Philistine in his forehead, that the stone sunk into his forehead; and he fell upon his face to the earth. So David prevailed over the Philistine with a sling and with a stone, and smote the Philistine, and slew him; but there was no sword in the hand of David."

EMPTY BOASTINGS

Goliath who was seemingly unchallengeable fell when he was challenged by the superior power of God. Many claims made many human beings collapse when they are challenged by God. Adolph Hitler, the strong man of Germany, once boasted that he would capture Africa and turn it into a rubber plantation. Where is Hitler now? His life ended in shame and disaster.

We have had Jesus of Oyingbo in this country before, who said in 1964, that he was God's incarnate and that he would not die. But he died long ago and without prior notice. Even now, some people are moving around the country calling themselves the Holy Spirit. A time would come when we would attend their funerals too, and we will be able to tell who the Holy Spirit is. Only one person, whose hands made an unchallengeable claim, stands today and will stand till eternity. That person is Jesus. **Matthew 28:16-18** confirms this:

"Then the eleven disciples went away into Galilee, into a mountain where Jesus had

---

appointed them. And when they saw him, they worshipped him: but some doubted. And Jesus came and spake unto them, saying, All power is given unto me in heaven and in earth."

It is a wonderful statement and only Jesus has successfully made that unchallengeable claim. The following Scriptures confirm this:

"Far above all principality, and power, and might, and dominion, and every name that is named, not only in this world, but also in that which is to come: and hath put all things under his feet, and gave him to be the head over all things to the church." **Ephesians 1:21-22**.

"Wherefore God also hath highly exalted him, and given him a name which is above every name: that at the name of Jesus every knee should bow, of things in heaven, and things in earth, and things under the earth." **Phil 2:9.**

THE UNCHALLENGING CLAIM

So, Jesus is power personified and at His name all other powers, with no apologies, have to bow. I dare you to name any power that has successfully challenged the power in the name of Jesus. Anyone challenging a Christian is challenging the unchallengeable. Jesus said, "all power" and not "some powers" has been given unto Him.

He did not say all powers in heaven alone. If He had said that, it would have suggested that the earth was excluded. He made it very clear by saying, "all power is given unto me in heaven and on earth." So, no power or person fighting against the gospel has ever progressed. We know the story of Emperor Nero, who fought against Christianity and killed many of the apostles. He died a miserable death. Today, the gospel is till alive and well.

WHEN GOD FIGHTS

Another French man called Voltaire boasted that he would devote the whole of his energy to destroy every Bible in France. He died and after his death printing was invented and a Christian press bought over his house and Bibles are now being printed there. If you are sure that you are a true child of God, do not bother yourself about your enemies who do not want to see you around or to prosper in all that you do. They are only challenging the unchallengeable. May be your enemies have been pursuing you or have converted the pursuit to a full time job, don't worry at all. For they are challenging the unchallengeable. Adolph Hitler hated Christianity with terrible passion, so much so that some people referred to him as the anti-Christ. He is now dead and his headquarters in Berlin is now a Christian chapel. Martin Bow, Hitler's lieutenant, was so anti-Christ that he called Christianity a poison and warned his wife never to allow his children to partake in Christianity. But his children refused to listen to him. And seven of the nine of them became Christians. One of them was even a missionary.

It is true that the devil may be controll ing most men, but the Bible says, "The earth is the Lord's and the fullness thereof." The Bible says, that for Him all things were created that are in heaven or that are on earth, whether visible or invisible, whether they be thrones or dominions or powers or principal ities. All things were created by Him and in Him all things consist. We thank God because Jesus is the same yesterday, today and forever.

When God rises and begins to fight on behalf of a Christian, no herbal ist can help the challenger. The moment you real ise that Jesus is your leader and your head and that He has all the powers, your d ifficulties will d isappear in His presence. All your problems will be solved. Your confusion will be removed. All your trials will eventually become triumphs and your temptations will become testimonies. Whoever challenges you henceforth is challenging the unchallengeable. I love that beautiful hymn which says, "Bruised is the serpent's head, hell has been vanquished, death is dead and Christ has gone up on high and captivity is made captive." I do not know the type of challenges that you are facing now. But it is clear that challenges are usually from four sources:

1. **The world.**
2. **Sin.**
3. **The flesh.**
4. **The devil.**

If the above-mentioned powers are challenging you, there is nothing you can do by your own power. But when you turn them over to the Lord they cannot challenge the unchallengeable. They will all fail and fall flat on their faces. The moment you recognise God as your head and trust in Him as well, you will begin to witness instant deliverance and instant miracles. The problem of many Christians is that they stay too long in the past that is why they still cry over things which happened to them long before they knew the Lord. It is therefore not difficult to see a 40-year old Christian crying over what happened to him or her at the age of 10. My advice to such people is to get out of such terrible state, lest they allow their past lives to ruin not only their present life, but the future as well. You need to forget your inglorious past.

PRESSING FORWARD
Apostle Paul said he was pressing forward successfully because he had forgotten his inglorious past. I plead with you again to stop living in the past. Don't forget that as a child of God you are a new creature and old things have passed away. Behold all things have become new. Make a quality decision now and get out of that situation, even if it means dying in trying to get out. It is better to die trying to get out of the back room the devil has locked you in than to remain alive there.

Please, make this confession now: "I refuse to stay in the back room. I am getting out, in Jesus' name." You will initiate the fight and then turn the challenger over to the Lord. That was exactly what David did. He went to look for trouble by accepting Goliath's challenge. Thereafter he handed Goliath over to the Lord. It was therefore easy for him to defeat Goliath. Elijah also went out to look for the trouble with the idol worshippers. He also ensured that there was no rain in the place for three and a half years. He locked up the heavens and put the keys in his pockets. God was happy about it and faithfully committed Himself to what he was saying.

TRUE VICTORY

Being a Christian does not give you automatic victory over many things. Victory comes when you identify your position in God. Thank God that He has made all things available for you. It is true that spiritual warfare is tough. It is not easy, but with the weapon that God has provided battles would be won easily. Many Christians will continue to live defeated lives until they rise up to fight like Esther did. Esther was not pleased about the way things were going for her people, so she went on three days fast. Thereafter, she declared, "If I perish, I perish." That was a woman who decided to move forward.

Do you know that God's promise is that ye shall not die but live to declare His works? When you begin to declare that, your challenger will know that you mean business. Don't continue to be in bondage to any problem or unfavourable situation. Decide now and declare this: "I am getting out of my problems today. You devil, you have been using depression and worry and anxiety against me. I am getting out today. Special announcement to all you demon and all your hosts: "I am getting out today, in Jesus' name."

DIVINE INTERVENTION

I used to have a good friend whose children fell sick everyday and she kept on spending money on them until they almost turned her to a pauper. When she could no longer afford the hospital bills, she turned her case over to God. She became born again and thereafter acquired necessary powers to put the enemies to shame. When the enemies saw her new position, they left her and her children alone. She had become an unchallengeable person.

Perhaps the devil is suffocating your physical and spiritual life and has taken you to a dangerous point. Perhaps your life has been turned upside down, or you are tired of life altogether. It is now time for you to get out. Declare boldly to the devil that you belong to Jesus. Tell him too that you are unchallengeable because your master Jesus is unchallengeable.

Know this and know it well, that if you do not resist the devil hard enough, he will not flee from you. Challenge him today, using the authority of Jesus and you will become free. God is waiting for you to do it. God will back you up and you will be free indeed.

PRAYER POINTS:

1. Let every satanic giant standing against me begin to fall after the order of Goliath, in the name of Jesus.
2. Let all diviners and enchanters hired against me fall after the order of Balaam, in the name of Jesus
3. Let all giants standing against peace and unity in my home fall and die, in Jesus' name.
4. I bind and set ablaze every sprit of marriage destruction, in Jesus' name.
5. Let all Pharaohs perish in the Red Sea, in the name of Jesus.
6. Let all my Herods be devoured by spiritual worms, in the name of Jesus.
7. Woe unto the spirits that turn into cows, elephants, masquerades or any other object in order to hinder my blessings, in the name of Jesus.

8. Lord, set my spirit on fire for You, in the name of Jesus..
9. Lord, fill me to brim with Your power, in the name of Jesus..
10. Let every architect of spiritual coffins enter therein themselves, in the name of Jesus.
11. I command the stronghold of fear, worry and anxiety to be pulled down in my life, in Jesus' name.
12. Let all drinkers of blood and eaters of flesh eat their own flesh and drink their own blood, in the name of Jesus.

OTHER BOOKS BY DR. D. K. OLUKOYA
1.   20 Marching Orders To Fulfill Your Destiny
2.   30 Things The Anointing Can Do For You
3.   30 Prophetic Arrows From Heaven
4.   A-Z of Complete Deliverance
5.   Abraham's Children in Bondage
6.   Basic Prayer Patterns
7.   Be Prepared
8.   Bewitchment must die
9.   Biblical Principles of Dream Interpretation
10.   Born Great, But Tied Down
11.   Breaking Bad Habits
12.   Breakthrough Prayers For Business Professionals
13.   Bringing Down The Power of God
14.   Brokenness
15.   Can God Trust You?
16.   Can God?
17.   Command The Morning
18.   Connecting to The God of Breakthroughs
19.   Consecration Commitment & Loyalty
20.   Contending For The Kingdom
21.   Criminals In The House Of God
22.   Dancers At The Gate of Death
23.   Dealing With The Evil Powers Of Your Father's House
24.   Dealing With Tropical Demons
25.   Dealing With Local Satanic Technology
26.   Dealing With Witchcraft Barbers
27.   Dealing With Unprofitable Roots
28.   Dealing With Hidden Curses
29.   Dealing With Destiny Vultures
30.   Dealing With Satanic Exchange

31. Dealing With Destiny Thieves
32. Deliverance Of The Head
33. Deliverance: God's Medicine Bottle
34. Deliverance From Spirit Husband And Spirit Wife
35. Deliverance From The Limiting Powers
36. Deliverance From Evil Foundation
37. Deliverance of The Brain
38. Deliverance Of The Conscience
39. Deliverance By Fire
40. Destiny Clinic
41. Destroying Satanic Masks
42. Disgracing Soul Hunters
43. Divine Yellow Card
44. Divine Prescription For Your Total Immunity
45. Divine Military Training
46. Dominion Prosperity
47. Drawers Of Power From The Heavenlies
48. Evil Appetite
49. Evil Umbrella
50. Facing Both Ways
51. Failure In The School Of Prayer
52. Fire For Life's Journey
53. For We Wrestle ...
54. Freedom Indeed
55. Healing Through Prayers
56. Holiness Unto The Lord
57. Holy Fever
58. Holy Cry
59. Hour Of Decision
60. How To Obtain Personal Deliverance
61. How To Pray When Surrounded By The Enemies

62.	I Am Moving Forward
63.	Idols Of The Heart
64.	Igniting Your Inner Fire
65.	Igniting Your Inner Fire
66.	Is This What They Died For?
67.	Kill Your Goliath By Fire
68.	Killing The Serpent of Frustration
69.	Let God Answer By Fire
70.	Let Fire Fall
71.	Limiting God
72.	Lord, Behold Their Threatening
73.	Madness Of The Heart
74.	Making Your Way Through The Traffic Jam of Life
75.	Meat For Champions
76.	Medicine For Winners
77.	My Burden For The Church
78.	Open Heavens Through Holy Disturbance
79.	Overpowering Witchcraft
80.	Paralysing The Riders And The Horse
81.	Personal Spiritual Check-Up
82.	Possessing The Tongue of Fire
83.	Power To Recover Your Birthright
84.	Power Against Coffin Spirits
85.	Power Against Unclean Spirits
86.	Power Against The Mystery of Wickedness
87.	Power Against Destiny Quenchers
88.	Power Against Dream Criminals
89.	Power Against Unclean Spirits
90.	Power Against Local Wickedness
91.	Power Against Marine Spirits
92.	Power Against Spiritual Terrorists

93. Power To Recover Your Lost Glory
94. Power To Disgrace The Oppressors
95. Power Must Change Hands
96. Power To Shut Satanic Doors
97. Power Against The Mystery of Wickedness
98. Power of Brokenness
99. Pray Your Way To Breakthroughs
100. Prayer To Make You Fulfill Your Divine Destiny
101. Prayer Strategies For Spinsters And Bachelors
102. Prayer Warfare Against 70 Mad Spirits
103. Prayer Is The Battle
104. Prayer To Kill Enchantment
105. Prayer Rain
106. Prayers To Destroy Diseases And Infirmities
107. Prayers For Open Heavens
108. Prayers To Move From Minimum To Maximum
109. Praying Against Foundational Poverty
110. Praying Against The Spirit Of The Valley
111. Praying In The Storm
112. Praying To Dismantle Witchcraft
113. Praying To Destroy Satanic Roadblocks
114. Principles Of Prayer
115. Raiding The House of The Strongman
116. Release From Destructive Covenants
117. Revoking Evil Decrees
118. Safeguarding Your Home
119. Satanic Diversion of the Black Race
120. Secrets of Spiritual Growth & Maturity
121. Seventy Rules of Spiritual Warfare
122. Seventy Sermons To Preach To Your Destiny
123. Silencing The Birds Of Darkness

124.	Slave Masters
125.	Slaves Who Love Their Chains
126.	Smite The Enemy And He Will Flee
127.	Speaking Destruction Unto The Dark Rivers
128.	Spiritual Education
129.	Spiritual Growth And Maturity
130.	Spiritual Warfare And The Home
131.	Stop Them Before They Stop You
132.	Strategic Praying
133.	Strategy Of Warfare Praying
134.	Students In The School Of Fear
135.	Symptoms Of Witchcraft Attack
136.	Taking The Battle To The Enemy's Gate
137.	The Amazing Power of Faith
138.	The Vagabond Spirit
139.	The Unlimited God
140.	The Wealth Transfer Agenda
141.	The Way Of Divine Encounter
142.	The Unconquerable Power
143.	The Baptism of Fire
144.	The Battle Against The Spirit Of Impossibility
145.	The Chain Breaker
146.	The Dinning Table Of Darkness
147.	The Enemy Has Done This
148.	The Evil Cry Of Your Family Idol
149.	The Fire Of Revival
150.	The School of Tribulation
151.	The Gateway To Spiritual Power
152.	The Great Deliverance
153.	The Internal Stumbling Block
154.	The Lord Is A Man Of War

155. The Mystery Of Mobile Curses
156. The Mystery Of The Mobile Temple
157. The Prayer Eagle
158. The University of Champions
159. The Power of Aggressive Prayer Warriors
160. The Power of Priority
161. The Tongue Trap
162. The Terrible Agenda
163. The Scale of The Almighty
164. The Hidden Viper
165. The Star In Your Sky
166. The star hunters
167. The Spirit Of The Crab
168. The Snake In The Power House
169. The Slow Learners
170. The Skeleton In Your Grandfather's Cupboard
171. The Serpentine Enemies
172. The Secrets Of Greatness
173. The Seasons Of Life
174. The Pursuit Of Success
175. Tied Down In The Spirits
176. Too Hot To Handle
177. Turnaround Breakthrough
178. Unprofitable Foundations
179. Victory Over Your Greatest Enemies
180. Victory Over Satanic Dreams
181. Violent Prayers Against Stubborn Situations
182. War At The Edge Of Breakthroughs
183. Wasted At The Market Square of Life
184. Wasting The Wasters
185. Wealth Must Change Hands

186.   What You Must Know About The House Fellowship
187.   When the Battle is from Home
188.   When You Need A Change
189.   When The Deliverer Need Deliverance
190.   When Things Get Hard
191.   When You Are Knocked Down
192.   When You Are Under Attack
193.   When The Enemy Hides
194.   When God Is Silent
195.   Where Is Your Faith
196.   While Men Slept
197.   Woman! Thou Art Loosed.
198.   Your Battle And Your Strategy
199.   Your Foundation And Destiny
200.   Your Mouth And Your Deliverance
201.   Your Mouth and Your Warfare

YORUBA PUBLICATIONS

1.   ADURA AGBAYORI
2.   ADURA TI NSI OKE NIDI
3.   OJO ADURA

FRENCH PUBLICATIONS

1. PLUIE DE PRIERE
2. ESPIRIT DE VAGABONDAGE
3. EN FINIR AVEC LES FORCES MALEFIQUES DE LA MAISON DE TON PERE
4. QUE l'ENVOUTEMENT PERISSE
5. FRAPPEZ l'ADVERSAIRE ET IL FUIRA
6. COMMENT RECEVIOR LA DELIVRANCE DU MARI ET FEMME DE NUIT
7. CPMMENT SE DELIVRER SOI-MEME
8. POVOIR CONTRE LES TERRORITES SPIRITUEL
9. PRIERE DE PERCEES POUR LES HOMMES D'AFFAIRES
10. PRIER JUSQU'A REMPORTER LA VICTOIRE
11. PRIERES VIOLENTES POUR HUMILIER LES PROBLEMES OPINIATRES
12. PRIERE POUR DETRUIRE LES MALADIES ET INFIRMITES
13. LE COMBAT SPIRITUEL ET LE FOYER
14. BILAN SPIRITUEL PERSONNEL
15. VICTOIRES SUR LES REVES SATANIQUES
16. PRIERES DE COMAT CONTRE 70 ESPIRITS DECHANINES
17. LA DEVIATION SATANIQUE DE LA RACE NOIRE
18. TON COMBAT ET TA STRATEGIE
19. VOTRE FONDEMENT ET VOTRE DESTIN
20. REVOQUER LES DECRETS MALEFIQUES
21. CANTIQUE DES CONTIQUES
22. LE MAUVAIS CRI DES IDOLES
23. QUAND LES CHOSES DEVIENNENT DIFFICILES

Dr. D.K Olukoya

ANNUAL 70 DAYS PRAYER AND FASTING PUBLICATIONS

1. Prayers That Bring Miracles
2. Let God Answer By Fire
3. Prayers To Mount With Wings As Eagles
4. Prayers That Bring Explosive Increase
5. Prayers For Open Heavens
6. Prayers To Make You Fulfil Your Divine Destiny
7. Prayers That Make God To Answer And Fight By Fire
8. Prayers That Bring Unchallengeable Victory And Breakthrough Rainfall Bombardments
9. Prayers That Bring Dominion Prosperity And Uncommon Success
10. Prayers That Bring Power And Overflowing Progress
11. Prayers That Bring Laughter And Enlargement Breakthroughs
12. Prayers That Bring Uncommon Favour And Breakthroughs
13. Prayers That Bring Unprecedented Greatness & Unmatchable Increase
14. Prayers That Bring Awesome Testimonies And Turn Around Breakthroughs

www.ingramcontent.com/pod-product-compliance
Lightning Source LLC
LaVergne TN
LVHW051201080426
835508LV00021B/2740